Wakanda Whooper

The Curious Cinnamon Crane

Wakanda Whooper

The Curious Cinnamon Crane

BY

SANDIA KOSMO

ILLUSTRATED BY LISA KOSMO

ISBN 13: 978-1-59298-713-9

Library of Congress Catalog Number: 2015920801

Printed on FSC-certified paper in the USA

First Printing: 2016
20   19   18   17   16   5   4   3   2   1

Cover and interior design by James Monroe Design, LLC.

Beaver's Pond Press, Inc.
7108 Ohms Lane
Edina, MN 55439–2129
(952) 829-8818
www.BeaversPondPress.com

Sandia Kosmo is available for bookstore signings, classroom visits, and speaking engagements. Visit www.wakandawhooper.com for more information.

I dedicate this book to the world's children,
our future.

To James,

A crane's peace,

Sandia Karma

When we hear the crane's call we hear no mere bird.
We hear the trumpet in the orchestra of evolution.

—ALDO LEOPOLD, "MARSHLAND ELEGY" IN *A SAND COUNTY ALMANAC*
WISCONSIN NATIVE AND FOUNDER OF THE DEPARTMENT OF WILDLIFE MANAGEMENT
AT THE UNIVERSITY OF WISCONSIN–MADISON IN 1939

My special thanks to Necedah National Wildlife Refuge manager Doug Staller and wildlife biologist Richard Urbanek (a.k.a. Dr. Crane) for their dedication and tremendous help with the research, maps, and factual information in this book.

I am grateful to the International Crane Foundation in Baraboo, Wisconsin, for maintaining the only place in the world where people can see all fifteen of the world's crane species, many of which are endangered. The site is near the Wisconsin River "shack" and land inhabited by Aldo Leopold when he wrote *A Sand County Almanac.*

I am grateful to the Indian Nations for their reverence of animals, especially the Ojibwe people and their Crane Clan, the Siouan people for their language with the name Wakanda, and the Ho-Chunk Nation surrounding the whooping cranes of Necedah for their care of land.

A portion of the proceeds from this book will return to the Necedah National Wildlife Refuge in Necedah, Wisconsin, and the International Crane Foundation in Baraboo, Wisconsin, to further the establishment of cranes east of the Mississippi River.

Wakanda (*wah-KAHN-da*) Whooper lives among tall pines, sturdy oaks, and grassy wetlands. Hatched at the Necedah (*neh-SEE-duh*) National Wildlife Refuge in central Wisconsin, this young whooping crane will join her family in being the tallest birds in North America—and among the tallest birds in the world.

Wakanda's parents, Papa and Mama Whooper, welcome their new little crane to their marshy refuge nest in the spring. About a foot wide and a foot deep, the little family's nest is made with mud and tall vegetation on the ground alongside Wisconsin's famous cranberry bogs. They give their newly hatched whooper a very special name—Wakanda, Wandy for short.

As they wade in the yellow-green marsh grass with its waters moving slowly toward the Wisconsin River, Mama Whooper tells Wandy, "The Sioux Indians say Wakanda means *mystical*. Here we're surrounded by the Ho-Chunk Indian Nation who once spoke a dialect of the Siouan language. They understand Wakanda to mean *earth keeper* or *mystical* also. It's the perfect name for you, our little whooper."

Papa adds, "Oh, Wandy, you were such a beautiful hatchling! We chose your name because we think you have a mystical power to help heal this earth. You will be part of making this earth beautiful, our little earth keeper. Indeed, you may possess the power to save us whooping cranes. We picked *Wakanda* just for you because you and the other new hatchlings here are the future for whooping cranes, but that future nearly wasn't possible. Little Wandy, you almost weren't hatched. You see, our whole extended whooper family almost died out. You and your fellow hatchlings inspired a joyous celebration for all the good people here hoping for a whooper comeback."

Wakanda fluffs out her soft, little cinnamon-colored feathers and listens carefully as Mama Whooper tells her more about her good fortune.

"Indians have clans or families named for animals like us. The Ojibwe people (or Chippewa)—an Indian nation that lives in northern Wisconsin, Minnesota, and Canada—think cranes are really important to our world," Mama Whooper says. "So important that they have a crane clan—their chieftains or spokespersons. When we whoopers speak, everyone for miles around can hear us. And in many places of the world, such as Japan, cranes are signs of healing and peace."

2

In her excitement, Wakanda slaps her feet in the muddy waters and dances around and around. "Wow, Mama, I love the meaning of my name! How wonderful that we are symbols of peace in the world. Thank you so much. I love you, and I love this place. I love it so much that I want to stay here forever."

Papa and Mama are startled by her words. They jerk back on their very long legs, almost tipping into the tall nest. They stare down at Wandy by craning their long, white necks.

"Oh, Wandy!" Papa exclaims. "We can't stay. Only a few animals live at this special place all year. Most of us leave in the fall. We're migrating birds—like the trumpeter swans and our cousins, the sandhill cranes. We can't stay here in Necedah for the winter."

Wakanda stretches her very long neck and turns to Papa with shock as her straight, long beak falls wide open.

Mama continues, "Necedah means 'Land of Yellow Waters,' which describes how the wetlands look in the spring, summer, and early fall."

After a long pause, Wandy finally blurts, "But why, Mama? I love this muddy, grassy playground. I have so much fun here with you and all the other animals. I play with my sandhill cousins, and we have fun hunting for food in the tall marsh grass."

Papa and Mama Crane strut around, deep in thought. They are elder cranes, and Wandy has noticed that the other birds in the marsh call them Doctor Mama and Doctor Papa Crane because they seem to know so much about crane history and wetland life. They appear to be the leaders of the whole flock. Their legs stretch up high in the grassy playground as they move in a circle around her. Finally, Mama breaks the silence.

"In late fall and winter, all of this looks like a collection of frozen skating rinks. We wouldn't survive without being able to hunt for insects and the other tasty treats we find in the summer waters."

"But we also have beautiful winter homes," Papa points out. "We go to them because we cannot find food and to escape the cold, cold winters here. Our whole extended crane family goes south for the winter. Just like some humans, we travel to a warmer place that doesn't have harsh winters and deep freezes."

Mama adds, "We need to go when the leaves turn red, yellow, and orange. We leave before snow covers the ground to announce winter."

Reluctant to accept the news but willing to tackle a new challenge, Wakanda lifts her sturdy beak, stretches out her soft cinnamon feathers, and declares, "Oh, yes, it will be fun to take a road trip and see new places."

So, flapping her huge wings, which startles the dragonflies around her, Wakanda decides to enjoy the whole summer and fall to the fullest. She eats insects, frogs, snakes, rodents, and other tasty treats from the wetlands. She grows larger and longer. As she explores the refuge marshes, she sees many other animals.

Wandy notices that her sandhill crane cousins like wading as much as her whooper family. The trumpeter swans float majestically on the beautiful waters beyond the marsh. Many times, she notices beautiful blue butterflies—Karner blue butterflies that, like she, are endangered. When Wandy practices flying, she encounters so many butterflies and birds on her refuge flights. They all clear the way as she lifts off with her majestic wings.

Wakanda loves everything about living in a home surrounded by the Ho-Chunk Indian Nation and cranberry bogs and kind people who watch from a distant shore, sometimes with binoculars. She knows she's going to miss this wonderful muddy, grassy playground, but Papa and Mama promise they'll all return in the spring.

Wakanda spends the warm summer days splashing and wading in the marsh. She meets other whoopers, but most of them are tall (very tall!) and white, not cinnamon like little Wandy. While the older, long-necked cranes whoop so loudly that the whole marsh can hear, she's more concerned about something else. She keeps dancing around and leaping up in a funny-looking, energetic dance, as if she's trying to shake off something.

Finally, with sadness in her little voice, she confesses her concern to her parents. "Why do I look like a cinnamon bear? You have such magnificent, long, white wings that look like the ends were dipped in black finger paint. Why don't I look like you? I keep trying to shake off these cinnamon feathers. Am I really an adopted sandhill crane instead of a whooping crane like you?" Looking up at Mama and Papa Whooper, she concludes her outburst with her biggest concern, "And I don't have that nice red cap on my head, either."

Mama's bright-yellow eyes light up as she turns her long, grayish-black beak toward her cinnamon-and-cream-colored daughter. She wants to laugh, but she knows Wandy is sincerely worried. "You're a young crane. Little cranes start with cinnamon feathers but lose them for white ones as they grow up—just like your sky-blue eyes will change to a radiant yellow by the end of summer. When you get older, you'll look just like us." Then Mama Whooper teases, "So you'll look like a crane-berry splatted all over your head too."

Wakanda and Papa Whooper laugh, slap their wings together, and leap high into the air.

"Don't you mean *cranberry*, Mama?" Wandy asks.

"No, Wandy, some humans say that when German settlers came to Wisconsin and saw the cranberry blossoms in the wetlands, they thought the flowers looked just like our heads and beaks. So they called them *craneberries*. Later, humans shortened the fruit name to *cranberries*. Some others say that we cranes loved cranberries so much that the little red berries were first called *craneberries*. Either way, they're definitely named after us. Those humans have big celebrations in Warrens, Eagle River, and Stone Lake, Wisconsin. You might say they *whoop it up* for the *craneberry*."

In honor of their namesake berry, Wandy and her parents dance around majestically, leap high in the air, and joyfully glide through the waters. Papa and Mama toss their heads back with beaks straight up and let out extremely loud whoops that can be heard for miles. Wandy tries to mimic them, but her whoops don't travel quite as far yet because her windpipe isn't as long or as developed yet.

Wakanda is thrilled to hear that she can expect to look like her parents one day with a cranberry cap. "Oh, Mama, you are so funny and so smart," Wakanda laughs.

4

Then Mama Whooper tells her little whooper some other wonderful news. "And, Wandy, you will be as tall as many humans. You will be all white with black-tipped wings. The skin on your head will show. It will be a lovely crown of bright cranberry red with no feathers where the crown comes in. You and your huge wings will soar with us wherever we go," Mama added.

Wakanda tries another whoop to celebrate. Then she turns her curious mind to another topic she's been thinking about. As they wade along the shore on their stilt-like legs and eat insects, Wandy stretches her long neck and turns her long beak toward Papa Whooper. "How did we get here in this great place with all these sturdy trees and this muddy, grassy playground?"

Papa Whooper turns his head, splashes his wing in the wetland water, and sweeps it out across the water. He turns his daggerlike beak toward Wandy as he considers. "Our ancestors, the whoopers who lived before us, were many more. They migrated from all across the vast area called Canada to places on the southern coast of the United States."

Papa pauses, giving Wakanda time to absorb his long explanation. "They and the sandhill cranes had many flyways, which are highways in the sky from north to south. Sometimes Canada geese would share the flyways with them."

Wakanda peers upward, trying to understand how there could be highways in the sky.

Papa Whooper continues, "There was one secret, faraway place in northern Canada that no one knew about except our ancestors. We were down to just one flyway from a time when there were more, all leading south. Each fall, our ancestor whoopers followed that last highway in the sky to the Texas coast, but each year, fewer and fewer whoopers made the trip. Finally, our ancestors were down to fewer than twenty whoopers making the migration flight. Our entire extended family was almost gone."

Wandy looks up with tears in her big, circle crane eyes and asks, "Oh, Papa, how did that happen?"

Papa chokes up and cannot continue. Mama Whooper picks up the story, telling Wandy about how whooping cranes disappeared by the hundreds from North America. "It was a very sad time. When they flew south to the ocean, Papa's grandparents couldn't find places to eat the foods we love—especially crunchy corn, tasty wetland and field insects, and those yummy blue crabs that we love from the ocean, our winter destination. Without enough food, many whoopers starved to death. It was a terrible time."

Papa Whooper's eyes well up with tears as his long neck bends down to the marsh. Mama continues, "Besides food problems, the survivors were having a hard time finding safe places to land during their flights to Texas. Many of the wetlands—what you call our muddy, grassy playgrounds, Wandy—were disappearing when humans built on top of them."

Wandy stomps her very long legs and feet in the wetlands mud in protest. Mud flies into the air and splats on the water. She grabs a floating stick and gives it a frustrated shake and flings it back into the yellow-blue water. "Oh, Mama and Papa, didn't humans see that we needed places to live too?"

"No, Wandy, they were more interested in places for themselves. So they filled in many of these wonderful wetlands for more and more houses and cities on dry land."

Wandy considers the tragic news of her ancestors. "So they couldn't find food or places to rest in those muddy, grassy playgrounds, Papa?"

"That's right, Wandy," Papa tells her. "Even worse, some hunters saw our ancestors as easy targets. The grayish-brown coloring of our sandhill cousins helps them sort of blend in, but we're bright white and so huge in the sky. Our wings spread out nearly eight feet. So hunters with guns shot our ancestors for trophies or for food."

Wakanda stomps her feet again and slams her large dagger beak into the marsh grass, almost getting it stuck. More mud flies as she tugs her beak out, lifts her cinnamon wings, and slaps them on the beautiful yellow-blue wetland waters. "No, Papa! No, no, no," she cries. "That is terrible news. What did your grandparents do?"

Papa shakes his head from side to side and tips it down very slowly, a gesture of great sadness.

Mama tells Wandy, "There was nothing they could do. Our family of majestic white fliers was doomed to die out, to go extinct. The tallest bird in North America would be no more."

6

Always curious and still hopeful, Wakanda tilts her tiny head with its long beak and adds, "But, Papa and Mama, we're still here. What happened? We're here now in this great place of serene ponds with tall, yellow-green grass that dances slowly over the clear, blue water just like we dance. We have plenty of food, especially those yummy insects and *craneberries*." They smile.

"Are we the only ones left?" Wandy continues.

Papa perks up at her question. He flips out his gigantic, black-tipped wings with enthusiasm, almost hitting a pileated woodpecker flying overhead. "No, we're just in a new home. Believe it or not, Wandy, a wonderful thing happened."

"What wonderful thing happened, Papa?" Wandy urges as she ruffles her cinnamon-and-cream feathers in expectation and leaps up out of the water and back, almost landing on a mallard duck floating nearby.

"It's a very surprising story," he answers, lifting his beak. Mama and Papa join in a unison call of celebration that makes the other wetland birds turn in surprise and fly off.

"Tell me now, Papa," Wakanda pleads, unable to stop fluttering her wings in excitement.

"Well, my little whooper, with only a tiny group of us whoopers left nesting in northern Canada, humans knew they had to do something quickly."

Wakanda looks puzzled and asks, "Mama, are we near that place in Canada now?"

"No, my little one," Mama replies with a flipping out of her huge black-tipped, white wings. "We're in a place—a state—called Wisconsin, far south and east of that early home in Canada. Remember, we're in a refuge called Necedah because of much help from humans."

"A refuge?" asks Wakanda.

"That's right, Wandy. Humans, the ones who caused our problems, decided they needed to help solve them. So they set aside certain areas just for animals and plants at risk of going extinct. Humans weren't allowed to hunt in certain parts of the refuge. Some humans made sure large areas of forest and wetlands were set aside for migrating birds like us and other animals, but we were free to go wherever we wanted, like now.

"Many humans work hard every day to keep the refuge as a perfect home for us with plenty of water and food. They have scientists called biologists who really care that we have a good place to thrive."

Wakanda claps her wings together and dances in the muddy water with her thin, long legs. "Wow, that's great. What else do these humans do?" she asks, and she continues dancing, especially enjoying the splashing slaps of her feet and wings on the water.

Papa smiles, proud to share the story of how their extended whooper family ended up in the refuge. "Besides setting apart these great refuges, people called *biologists* tried many times to help us survive. They didn't know if their plan would work. They started in Idaho with our smaller cousins, the sandhill cranes. There were many more of them from the very beginning. In fact, scientists found evidence that they existed in prehistoric times. They thought the sandhill flock could and would nurture our eggs. The experiment didn't work. The biologists tried many other things but without success. They had to find another plan to save us—and quickly—because we were almost extinct."

7

Suddenly, Mama Whooper lets out an extremely loud warning call. Every bird in the refuge is on high alert. The other whoopers, sandhills, and even the tundra swans and ducks start moving deeper into the refuge water more quickly than usual.

"Mama," Wandy cries, "what's wrong? I thought we're safe here."

"Just keep gliding with all of us, and don't stop to look back. I'll tell you while we move farther into the wetlands."

Every water animal was disappearing deeper into the wetlands grass. Mama Whooper finally declares, "I spied a raccoon near the shoreline. They think we make tasty snacks, especially smaller whoopers like you. We must stay clear of them," she stresses. "If we move deeper into the wetlands, they don't usually follow us."

As all the fliers move to deeper waters, Mama pierces the stillness with an even more terrifying alert that resounds through the whole refuge again. This time, even the threatening raccoon is alarmed and retreats into the forest from the water's edge.

"Are raccoons the only creatures we should fear?" asks Wandy.

"No," Papa declares. "We must watch for coyotes, red foxes, badgers, even eagles. So even though we're safer here than other places, we have enemies—or predators—that will attack us. Especially a lone whooper."

"Oh, Papa and Mama, I'll keep watch wherever I go so I can warn everyone about those animals too."

"Just be on your guard, Wandy. The whole refuge is safe again after Mama's loud warning calls to everyone," Papa says, smiling.

Everyone settles in for a peaceful night under the stars and a full moon, the second in the month, which means it's a blue moon.

8

"Now that we're safe again, let's get back to our story, Wandy," Mama encourages.

Papa perks up.

"Oh, Papa, time was really running out to save us! With so few of us whoopers left, what plan did they think up that would work?" Wakanda prompts.

"These crane-loving humans thought they could help some of us start a new life in a new place, Wandy. They picked Wisconsin for the start of a second flyway. That would ensure that, if something happened to our very small family flock of whoopers flying from northwestern Canada to the Gulf Coast in Texas, there would still be whoopers in another place—*this* place. This new flock would have different winter and summer locations farther east, east of the Mississippi River," Papa tells her.

Wakanda looks at Papa with a very puzzled turn of her large, long beak. "I'm curious again, Papa and Mama. How could humans possibly help us? Weren't they the ones who were taking over our wetlands and shooting us?"

"Yes, Wandy," Papa and Mama Whooper chime in chorus. "But it's strange. When we were almost all gone, they thought of one last thing. They wanted so much to save us tall, beautiful birds before we disappeared from the earth like so many other birds. Besides us very rare whoopers, this refuge also protects the endangered Karner blue butterflies and the Kirtland's warblers."

Wakanda freezes. "Oh, Mama, oh, no, no. You mean other birds disappeared?" she cries.

"Wandy," Mama consoles, "many different birds—like passenger pigeons, Carolina parakeets, and ivory-billed woodpeckers—have disappeared from the earth. They could no longer find food or shelter because humans put buildings where they lived, hunters shot at some of them, and sometimes pesticides poisoned the fields where they ate."

Wakanda flops down in the water at this news. Slapping the water with one cinnamon wing, she replies, "No, no. What are these *pesticides*?"

Papa stretches his long neck, getting ready to explain the strange word. He starts, "Pesticides are chemicals that keep insects from eating the plants, which helps the plants grow bigger and stronger. Some are good, but some of the chemicals can poison the food in the ground and the water that flows into wetlands and streams."

Wakanda looks up sadly, "So do some chemicals poison us, Papa?"

"We aren't sure, but these human scientists watch and protect us in this place and other refuges, Wandy."

"Oh good, Papa," Wakanda says, perking up. "So things are better for us now?"

9

"Well," Mama interjects, "our lives are better because of these special refuges for just us birds, other animals, and special plants. We do need the farmers' grains when we travel and take lodging in farm fields and refuges. I'm sorry to tell you, but we had another huge problem."

Turning her beak aside and shaking it back and forth, Wandy screeches, "Oh no! How can there be so many problems for one bird family, Mama? I don't know if I can hear one more."

"It's about our homes," Papa tells her. "Remember, those few surviving whoopers knew of only one safe place to live in Canada and only one safe place to stay in Texas during the winters. That was it."

He continues, "It took humans years and years to find where our ancestors nested up north in Canada. It's a place called Wood Buffalo National Park that's far, far north in northern Alberta, Canada. Humans knew we needed another place because drought or hurricanes in Texas where we wintered could kill off every last one of us. Or an illness called a virus might kill the only small flock left."

Mama adds, "That's when some good humans found us this new home in Wisconsin."

Then Wakanda has a dreadful thought. "But I don't understand how we fly south and know where to go if this is new territory."

Papa tweaks his beak at Wandy's good comment and replies, "The first year of this new eastern flyway was 2001. We had no idea where to go for the winter. Of course, our whooper family had heard of the Texas flyway from Canada, but not this new one from Wisconsin to Florida. Those clever human biologists were always thinking. They came up with an amazing plan to save us and show us the way to a new home for the winter that is far east of Texas."

Wakanda flutters her wings and dances around with relief. "Oh good, Papa," she says, smiling. "What was it?"

"They took some of our newly laid eggs from that homeland way up north in Canada," pipes up Mama Whooper. "That's how the comeback started, how your Papa and I started. These days, these kind scientists hatch eggs in many places, such as San Antonio in Texas, New Orleans in Louisiana, Calgary in Alberta, Canada, and in the eastern state of Maryland. Many eggs are hatched with human help. And better yet, we have this wetland home where you were hatched. We are a family and will fly together. But in our history, some of us whoopers joined their flocks in a different way to keep us from going extinct."

As Mama, Papa, and Wandy wade deeper into the refuge for the night, Mama Whooper adds, "Mama whoopers usually lay two eggs."

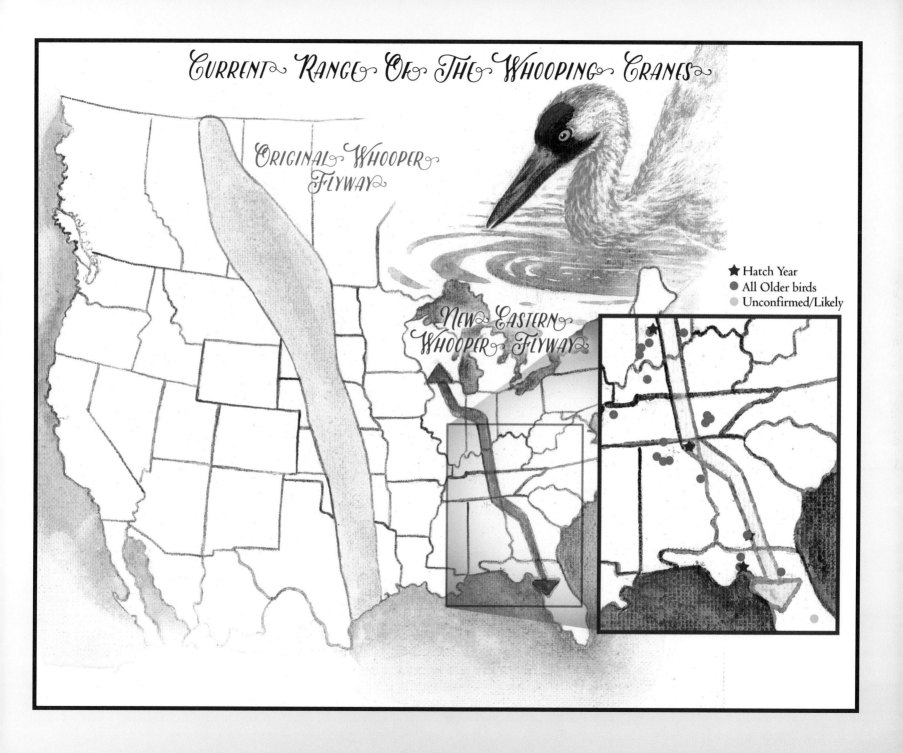

CURRENT RANGE OF THE WHOOPING CRANES

ORIGINAL WHOOPER FLYWAY

NEW EASTERN WHOOPER FLYWAY

★ Hatch Year
● All Older birds
● Unconfirmed/Likely

Papa continues, "It is hard for crane parents to find food for one baby whooper and very hard to find enough food for two babies. The stronger little whooper usually lives, and sadly, the other one often dies. So when humans took one egg from some of the nests far north in Canada, it was good for the egg left in the nest and good for the one taken to hatch at a special care place. It was a win-win."

"At first, the humans took the extra eggs to a place even farther east of this refuge," Mama adds. "It's called Patuxent (*pah-TUHKS-unt*) Wildlife Research Center in Maryland. Once there, nice people took very good care of these extra eggs until they hatched into baby cranes. When the babies were strong enough, these caring people sent the little cranes—or colts, as they call them—to this great place they found for us in Wisconsin. That's how the whooping cranes' comeback started here. And that's where I was hatched."

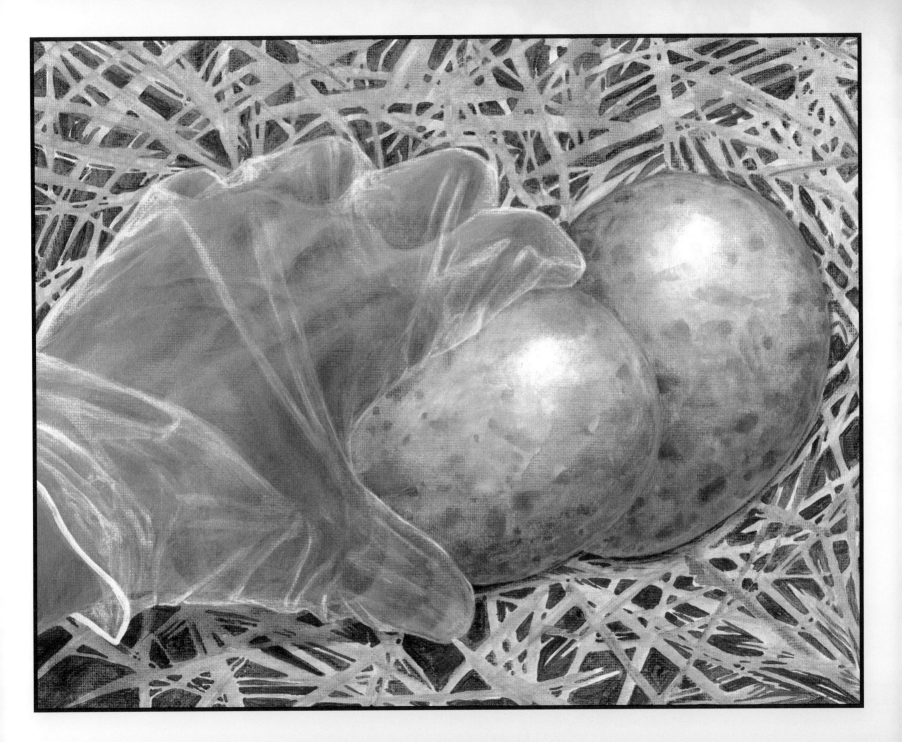

10

Curiosity overtakes Wakanda again. "Okay, how did those little whoopers survive without mamas and papas to feed them until they were old enough to be on their own?"

"Wandy, the kind humans found these really huge birds to take care of the baby whoopers as they grew to be fledglings, or birds that could fly. The huge birds that feed them are as tall as we are. Some are even taller than our five feet, but they are much wider than we are. They are white, like adult whoopers. They feed the little whoopers grains and grapes to make them strong. They use a puppet that looks like our beak to feed the little ones. These large birds are silent most of the time, but once in a while, they whoop loudly like we do. Our very loud whooping call is how we got our name, you know. We are loud whoopers." Papa and Mama let out one of their unison calls.

"Were the big birds cranes too, Papa?" Wandy asks.

"I don't think so. I watched them for many days," Papa tells Wandy. "Finally, I realized they were humans in costumes, but none of the other cranes figured it out except your smart mama. These huge birds can't fly, probably because they're thicker around their middle than we are—and they have thick legs and great big feet too. They're in costume, though, because they don't want the little whoopers to rely on humans. They want them to be with our own whoopers. They don't want the baby whoopers they raise to *imprint* on them, which means take them as parents. When the humans are in the crane costumes, the baby whoopers see them as just big, kind whoopers."

Mama adds, "The giant birds were so caring all the time. They seemed to truly love our little flock of cinnamon cranes. They cared for us like family."

"You know what, Wandy?" Papa asks. "That help included showing the first whoopers here in Necedah a highway in the sky to fly south for the winter."

Wandy stomps her two feet in frustration and sticks her long beak straight up in the air, coming down hard on the marsh water. "But, Papa, I don't understand at all. You said they couldn't fly. How could they teach those little cranes to follow them south for the winter if they themselves couldn't fly?"

11

"These kind bird people had one more surprise for us," Papa whoops.

Trying to whoop it up like Papa, Wakanda exclaims, "Oh, Papa and Mama, I love surprises! What was it?"

All three whoopers dance and leap and whoop as the moonlight catches their shadows on the water. The carrying on draws the attention of the animals in the marsh, who watch in curiosity at the three-whooper display.

"Oh, my little Wandy, I bet you thought the giant bird people were the biggest surprise, but no," Mama teases. "It was an even bigger bird than the giant bird people that fed us little whoopers. It was like those giant, shiny, silver birds called airplanes we see flying in the sky, but this one looked like a huge bird. But they're really just airplanes with lighter wings painted to look like ours with a giant bird person inside to lead the way by flying the huge bird plane. Humans copied the sturdy, huge wings that lift us into the sky to make what they call an ultralight aircraft. All the young cinnamon whoopers were sure it was a parent bird that looked like us adults."

Wakanda asks curiously, "Okay, so their wings looked like ours. But what could the giant bird plane do to help the little whoopers?"

Papa begins dancing around majestically once more. "That's the wonderful part of our story," he notes. "The giant bird plane would fly up into the air over the refuge and get the little cinnamon whoopers like you to follow. Then it would lead us around the area and back to the refuge and safety. It didn't take us long to figure out that flying was a good idea and that it was so much fun to play that way in the refuge. So there we were, flying up with the ultralight and then back down to the refuge, up and back, up and back, thinking it was just a gigantic crane parent. Following this giant flier all around the neighborhood and then landing back here was really fun for us."

"But, Papa, you said we couldn't stay here through the cold winters to play and fly up and down, up and down. These yellow-blue ponds we're standing in will freeze over. Our food will be covered with deep snows. Mama said we can't walk in the water because it will be a bunch of skating rinks in the winter."

Mama can't contain herself. Before Papa can respond, she says, "That's right, Wandy. So this is the biggest surprise of all. One day in late fall that first year, the little cinnamon whoopers took off with the huge bird plane, but they didn't come back to the refuge."

"Oh, no, don't tell me! Something bad happened again!" Wakanda screeches. "That's a horrible surprise."

"No, Wandy," Papa reassures her. "For once, nothing bad happened. It was just the opposite. It was a very good thing. The bird plane kept leading that first flock south for miles and miles through many states. The little ones just kept following and trusting the bird plane would lead them to safety. These little fliers flung their legs back and flapped their gigantic cinnamon-and-cream wings."

Wakanda can't contain her curiosity. Questions race to her mind. "Papa, that's wonderful! Was the journey long? Did you and the other cranes get tired? Where did you sleep? How did you find food?"

"The journey took many, many days, Wandy. The first group led by the ultralight in 2001 flew many miles each day. We touched down in other refuges on the way south to get food, shelter, and sleep. Sometimes we stopped in the fields of kind farmers. Many times, humans gathered on the ground and cheered us and the other little cinnamon birds on. Humans were so surprised and delighted to see us."

Mama piped up with a tweak of her beak, "They were whooping it up for us whoopers—for our comeback and our new flyway south for the winter. They were so happy to see these young cinnamon whoopers flying strong to a winter home. After flying through many states—Illinois, Indiana, Kentucky, Tennessee, Mississippi, Alabama, and Georgia—that bird plane led us to the Gulf Coast shores of Florida."

Mama added, "In more recent years, some of the whoopers find homes along the way and stay in those places instead. Others fly the distance to the Florida ocean shores, where there are beautiful ocean waters for wading and plenty of yummy blue crabs, our favorite southern shore lunch that's a break from our favorite northern lunch—berries, grains, and insects."

12

As summer turns to fall, the days turn cooler and shorter. Leaves start falling from the trees just like Mama said they would. The winds take on a fierce chill. Wandy knows her parents are preparing for that sky trip south with all the other whooper families.

Papa informs Wandy, "The three of us will be doing the full trip without the ultralight bird plane but with other whooper families. We are flying to a really neat Florida refuge with an ocean view."

"So, Mama, you said that place is many days of flying through many states. How do you know the way without the plane leading you? And how do you and the other cranes get back to this wonderful refuge when spring comes again?"

"After that first ultralight flight, we could do it on our own every year and in much less time. The route became a new flyway, an unmarked highway in the sky that we remember forever. We whoopers have an excellent sense of direction—and a great memory. We follow the same route year after year with older whoopers leading the way instead of an ultralight now. We do have to watch out for power lines, so we try to fly very high in the sky."

Mama dances, flipping up one wing and then the other as she jokes, "Is it a bird? Is it a plane?" Then she sticks up both wings at the same time. "It took a combined bird plane to start our migration! But now it is only us whooping cranes flying high and growing in numbers. We are superbirds of survival."

As the three whooper family members dance and dance, gracefully leaping into the air occasionally, Wakanda laughs. "Funny, Mama. I see now. Humans figured out that they had to fix what they made go wrong, and they did it just in time for us whoopers. If humans and animals work together," she reflects, "we can all live in a beautiful world that's good for humans and animals alike."

Together, Papa and Mama Whooper let out one big unison whoop for the whooping crane families saved in North America and the happy story of their great whooping crane family. Their joint whoop can be heard for miles.

"When we get to the new refuge," Mama promises, "we really whoop it up and dance all over, celebrating that there are enough wetlands and enough food for the whole whooper flock."

Wakanda exclaims, "I'm so happy I'm a whooping crane with homes in these two wonderful places! When do we take off for Florida? I want to try those blue crabs for a shore lunch when we get there!"

"We're ready to take off, Wandy. Then we'll return here to our muddy, grassy playground in Wisconsin next spring," Papa reminds her.

"Let's go find that highway in the sky to our winter home," Wakanda says. She flaps her huge wings, flips back her long, thin legs, and points her very long beak south as the whole Necedah whooper flock lifts off for their winter home with her happy family.

The end
Whoop it up for whoopers!

ACTIVITIES

www.WakandaWhooper.com

Wakanda's Song

Lyrics by Sandia Kosmo; music by Jonathan Meier
(website has guitar and piano music and Jon's rendition of the song:
www.wakandawhooper.com)

We see those whoopers in the sky,
A gorgeous scene as they fly high.
We hear those whoopers in the sky,
And whoop ourselves as they fly by.

Hatched in the refuge one May day,
Wakanda danced in the sun's ray,
Among whoopers born wild once more
New eastern homes to the Gulf shore.

Chorus:
Wakanda's spirit fills the air,
She bids a crane's peace everywhere.
Wakanda's spirit fills the air.

So few there were who nested north,
But humans came and brought them forth.
Now they fly from their wetland post
In Wisconsin to the Gulf Coast.

North America's tallest bird,
For miles, their loud whoop can be heard.
They spread those wings out seven feet
That highway in the sky to greet.

Chorus

May cranes be ever with our earth,
And whoop their comeback with great mirth.
Thanks be to humans and their care.
One day whoopers will not be rare.

Chorus

Sandia Kosmo

Jonathan Meier

Every land where cranes appear has tales and myths about the cranes,
which since ancient times have represented longevity
and good fortune, harmony and fidelity.

—PETER MATTHIESSEN, *THE BIRDS OF HEAVEN: TRAVELS WITH CRANES*, 2001

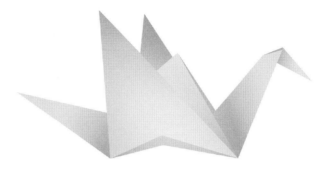

Learn about and Make an Origami Crane

In Japan and other places, the crane is a sign of healing and peace. A young girl named Sadako survived the bombing of Hiroshima, Japan, at the end of World War II but developed leukemia from the radiation. She worked to fold one thousand cranes in order to receive her wish of a full recovery, as legend maintains, for those who fold that many cranes. She didn't live long enough to reach her goal, but in Hiroshima Peace Memorial Park, the Children's Peace Monument bears the following inscription that honors her:

> *"This is our cry, this is our prayer:*
> *for building peace in the world."*

On the website www.thousandcranes.net, you will find ways to make cranes using various papers, including discarded gift-wrapping paper. This site and others share many ideas for putting cranes together for a necklace, wreath, or other types of display. It also offers information on sending origami cranes to the Children's Peace Monument honoring Sadako in Japan.

Visit a Whooper Home

Necedah National Wildlife Refuge in Necedah, Wisconsin, is east of Tomah and west of Necedah on State Trunk Highway 21. Interactive exhibits and a gift shop are in the visitor center. Walking trails and observation areas surround the center. Visitors can pick up self-guided walking tour maps, and guided school class tours can be scheduled (www.fws.gov/refuge/necedah).

Horicon National Wildlife Refuge in Mayville, Wisconsin, is northeast of Madison and northwest of Milwaukee. Similar to Necedah, tours are encouraged. This refuge is another crane raising place (www.fws.gov/refuge/horicon/).

International Crane Foundation just outside Baraboo, Wisconsin, has living species of all fifteen cranes from around the world, including the whooping crane. Guided tours and a visitor center are available (www.savingcranes.org).

Visit Aldo Leopold Sites

Aldo Leopold Legacy Center in Baraboo, Wisconsin, is operated by the Aldo Leopold Foundation; the center is northeast of Baraboo at E13701 Levee Road. There you can take a guided tour of the shack where Aldo Leopold wrote the classic land ethic book, *A Sand County Almanac* (1949). Several quotes from that book are cited in this book (www.aldoleopold.org).

Aldo Leopold Nature Center in Monona, Wisconsin, is next to Madison and offers workshops, displays, and more. (www.aldoleopoldnaturecenter.org).

Go to a Crane Festival

In the second week of September each year, Green Lake County, Wisconsin, has a free-admission crane festival. It includes activities for all ages: kids' arts and crafts, food, speakers, vendor booths, exhibits, and a trip to the Necedah NWR for a small fee. Check for reservations on tours. For more information, visit www.cityofprincetonwi.com.

The International Crane Foundation holds a festival in Baraboo, Wisconsin, in early August each year. The festival includes tours to see the fifteen live crane species, nature walks, and special programs and speakers. For more information, visit www.savingcranes.org.

Cranberry festivals in Wisconsin take place in Eagle River, Stone Lake, and Warrens. Their activities are similar to the ones listed above and emphasize the whoopers' namesake, the crane-berry.

*"I will write peace on your wings,
and you will fly all over the world."*

—Sadako Sasaki, age 12, Hiroshima, Japan

GLOSSARY

Alberta, Canada: a province of western Canada (a province is similar to a state in the United States). The original flock of whooping cranes nests there in the spring at The Wood Buffalo National Park of Canada.

biologists: scientists who study living plants and animals, often in the species' native environments.

blue moon: a second full moon within the month—despite its name, it isn't actually blue, but it is rare.

Chassahowitzka National Wildlife Refuge: known as "Chaz," a refuge on the Gulf Coast of Florida north of Tampa where some of the whooping cranes spent the winter until 2013 (www.fws.gov/chassahowitzka).

colt: young crane, also called a chick.

cranberry bog: a marshy area set aside to grow the red cranberry (craneberry), one of three fruits native to North America. First harvested by First Americans (Indians).

craning: an expression that describes turning one's neck to see. This phrase comes from the crane and its extremely long neck.

dialect: a version or form of a language that is peculiar to a specific region or social group.

endangered: a term used to describe a species near extinction

extinct: a species that has gone out of existence.

fledgling: a whooping crane that has reached the age in which it can fly.

Ho-Chunk Indian Nation: Once called the Winnebago Nation, the natives returned to their original language name in 1994. They inhabit much of the area of central Wisconsin that surrounds Necedah National Wildlife Refuge and ranges to southern Wisconsin. Many of the place names in the area are from their Siouan language, including Necedah.

Horicon National Wildlife Refuge: Located in Mayville, which is northeast of Madison and northwest of Milwaukee, Wisconsin, this refuge has whooping cranes and the largest freshwater cattail marsh in the United States. Open year round, the refuge offers wildlife viewing, hiking, bicycling, fishing and hunting (www.fws.gov/refuge/horicon/).

imprint: to recognize another animal or human as a trusted parent.

Japan: an Asian country that reveres the crane as a symbol of healing and peace, and the site of the Children's Peace Monument in Hiroshima.

migrating birds: birds that have a set flyway from north to south for the winter and south to north for the summer. They return to the same summer and winter homes every year.

Necedah: Ho-Chunk name meaning "land of yellow waters" because of the tawny-yellow water stained by soil minerals.

Necedah National Wildlife Refuge: a forty-four-thousand-acre area in central Wisconsin, near Tomah, that was established in 1939 by President Franklin D. Roosevelt as a breeding ground for migratory birds and other wildlife, including the endangered whooping crane, the Kirtland's warbler, and the Karner blue butterfly. The refuge includes wetlands, prairie, sedge meadow, pine-oak forest, and savannah. Refuge activities include hiking, hunting in designated areas, fishing, and attending children's and adult educational and interpretive programs (www.fws.gov/refuge/necedah).

Ojibwe (Chippewa) Indian Nation: located in northern Wisconsin, Minnesota, and Canada, their spokesperson chieftain clan is represented by the whooping crane. They also call themselves the Anishinaabe.

pesticides: substances used to kill, repel, or control certain forms of plant or animal life that are considered pests—for example, insects that eat farmers' crops or weeds in a lawn.

predator: an animal that preys on other animals.

prehistoric times: a time before written records.

refuge: a place set aside for the preservation of plants and animals, especially migrating birds and butterflies.

St. Mark's National Wildlife Refuge: located on the Gulf Coast of Florida 25 miles south of Tallahassee, it has become another location for whooping cranes to migrate for the winter months. Established in 1931, it is well known for its migratory bird population. St. Mark's is an excellent place for bird watching (www.fws.gov/refuge/aransas). The whoopers enjoy catching blue crabs there, just as they do in the Aransas National Wildlife Refuge in Texas (www.fws.gov/chassahowitzka).

scientists: persons working in a systematic way to acquire knowledge.

Siouan language: language of Woodland and Plains Indian nations, including the Missouri Valley, Mississippi Valley (Mandan, Dakota, Lakota, Nakota), the Chiwerean (Chiwere-Iowa, Otoe, Missouria), and the Wisconsin Ho-Chunk, among others with various dialects of the base language.

ultralight aircraft: a small, light, one-person airplane.

virus: a transmittable illness.

Wakanda: this word or a variation of Wakanda is found in Ho-Chunk, Omaha-Ponca Sioux, Lakota Sioux, and other Siouan languages. It means *mystical, earth keeper, Great Spirit,* or *the sacred mystery.* The Omaha-Ponca word is "Wakanda." The Lakota Sioux expression is "Wakan Tanka." The Ho-Chunk (Hocak) word is "Wau-con-chunk," according to the Wisconsin Historical Society and language vocabulary recorded by fur trader Henry Merrell.

Wood Buffalo National Park of Canada in Alberta, Canada, and the Northwest Territory: far northwesterly Canadian site where the whooping cranes nest in the western flyway and lay their eggs. It is Canada's largest national park. General Park site: (www.pc.gc.ca).

WHOOPING CRANE TRIVIA

Scientific name: *Grus americana*

Height: 5 feet, making it the tallest bird in North America

Weight: Female, 14 pounds; male, 16 pounds

Wing span: 7.5 feet

Longevity: 22 to 30 years in the wild; 31 to 40 years in captivity

Color: Adult is white with black wing tips, yellow eyes, and a bare red face and head, while young cranes (under one year old) are cinnamon-and-cream colored with blue eyes for the first three months

Colts: Young cranes; they are also called chicks

Stride: Moves about a yard with each stride

Whoops: Calls can carry two miles or more due to the long windpipes of whooping cranes

Guard call: Whoopers have a strong sense of community and emit a guard call to warn others when a predator is near.

Unison call: Male and female adults call together, stretching their beaks straight up and close to one another. They do this unison call in the morning, after waking, as part of courtship, and when defending their territory. Females have a two-note call; males have a single-note call.

Diet: Whoopers are omnivores. They eat both small animals and plants: worms, snakes, crustaceans, frogs, insects, grains, nuts, fruit, roots, and tubers (for example, potatoes).

Eggs: In April or May, female whooping cranes lay one or two greenish-gray eggs that are about 2.5 by 4 inches.

Tracking: Scientists fit whooping cranes with electronic bands on their legs to keep track of their movements. For the sake of aesthetic quality in the artwork, the author and illustrator of this book chose to leave the bands off the birds.

2001: The year the first seven fledglings followed an ultralight plane to a winter home in Florida. Five survived the winter and returned to Necedah in Wisconsin. (Bobcats in Florida have killed several cranes, but relocating the bobcats has helped.)

June 22, 2006: Two wild whooping cranes were hatched in Necedah National Wildlife Refuge. They were the first two whoopers to hatch naturally in the midwestern United States in over one hundred years.

2014: Endangered Species Recovery Champion Award 2014 to Necedah National Wildlife Refuge. The award recognizes staff and their efforts at conserving whooping cranes, Karner blue butterflies, and Kirtland's warblers. "Their contributions within the refuge and beyond are examples of sound scientific application and adaptive management," the award states.

Acknowledgments

Doug Staller, manager, Necedah National Wildlife Refuge

Richard Urbanek, wildlife biologist, Necedah National Wildlife Refuge

International Crane Foundation, Baraboo, Wisconsin

Horicon National Wildlife Refuge, Mayville, Wisconsin

The Indian Nations, especially the Ho-Chunk, Ojibwe, and Omaha-Ponca and Lakota Sioux

United States Fish & Wildlife Service

Wisconsin Department of Natural Resources, Madison, Wisconsin

Wisconsin Historical Society, Madison, Wisconsin

Linda Aaseng, reviewer

Sonja Disa Christoffersen, reviewer

Jennee Christoffersen Hancock, reviewer

Jim Kosmo, reviewer, brother, and author of *Still Standing*

Steve Kosmo, reviewer

Jonathan Meier, "Wakanda's Song" music

John Moseng, reviewer

Elaine Welin, website designer and Facebook page designer

Beaver's Pond Press, Edina, Minnesota

May cranes be ever with our earth
and whoop their comeback with great mirth . . .
Wakanda's spirit fills the air.
She bids a crane's peace everywhere.

—Wakanda's Song, Sandia Kosmo

"I am the same height as an adult whooper!"

About the Author

Sandia (Sandee) Kosmo is a native of Eau Claire, Wisconsin. She grew up at the typewriter of her mother Virginia Kosmo, who was a correspondent for the *St. Paul Pioneer Press* and the *Milwaukee Journal*. Sandee is first a writer whose passion for prose and poetry has taken her in many directions. She has served as a journalist, a high school and college teacher, a public relations specialist, a college director, and a Lutheran and United Church of Christ (UCC) ordained pastor. Sandee has a BA in English and journalism from UW-Eau Claire, Wisconsin; an MS in audio visual education from UW-Stout, Menomonie, Wisconsin; and an MDiv in theology from Luther Seminary, St. Paul, Minnesota.

After several years in New Mexico, she retired and returned to Wisconsin. Like whooping cranes, she migrates south for the winter. Sandee has two adult daughters, Jennee (Peter) Hancock and Sonja Christoffersen (Adam Donovan), and one grandson Dillon James Hancock.

About the Illustrator

Lisa Perrin Kosmo was born in Munsan-ri, South Korea. She received a BFA from the College of Visual Arts in St. Paul. Artists that she is inspired by include: Georgia O'Keeffe, Salvador Dali, Rabbett Before Horses, Frank Howell, and Peter Paul Rubens. Her art is a reflection of her multicultural ethnicity and she is a member of the Red Cliff Band, Ojibwe Nation in Bayfield, Wisconsin. Lisa lives in northeastern Minnesota with her husband and two sons.

ABOUT THE MUSICIAN

Jonathan Meier is a guitarist and composer from Eau Claire, Wisconsin. He holds a bachelor's degree in Jazz Performance from the University of Wisconsin-La Crosse. After school he spent six months with a cruise ship show band before moving to his current home of Minneapolis, Minnesota. Jonathan can be found as a sideman in cover bands, jazz groups, and pit orchestras. When he isn't playing music, he can be found playing soccer, running, or walking along the Mississippi River.